International
Cooking Collection

Healthy Food
for Kids
Carole Handslip

CONTENTS

Published exclusively for Cupress (Canada) Ltd
20 Torbay Road, Markham, Ontario L3R 1G6 Canada
by Woodhead-Faulkner (Publishers) Ltd, Simon & Schuster International Group

This edition first published 1988
© Woodhead-Faulkner (Publishers) Ltd 1988
All rights reserved
ISBN 0-920691-47-1
Printed and bound in Italy

INTRODUCTION

Although obesity among children may be on the increase, most children look healthy and far less in need of a change in diet than their parents. And it isn't easy to convince them that the effects of bad eating will tell when they reach the unimaginable age of forty! So, any approach to healthy eating for children must be logical and the food should be attractive and very tasty.

For children to adopt a healthy diet we need to encourage them to eat more fresh fruit and vegetables, pulses and unrefined foods, at the expense of refined foods—especially sugar—and those foods which contain additives. It is also a good idea to cut down on animal sources of fat, such as butter, cream, full-fat cheese and red meat.

Refined foods have tremendous taste appeal with children, so it isn't easy to introduce healthier alternatives. But try making your own spreads and sauces and look out for the ever-increasing number of wholefoods and additive-free convenience foods available in supermarkets.

For young children it helps to give healthy food a novelty appeal. Whole wheat scones for instance may not raise squeals of delight, but scone moons, stars and pigs will go down a treat. A sandwich train will also make your children's eyes light up, and you can easily sneak a healthy filling inside.

A word of warning, however: one certain way of putting your children off is to force them into eating foods they simply don't enjoy. Equally it is impossible to control what your child eats while away from home, so relax and let common sense turn your diet into a workable eating pattern for your children. The recipes and suggestions on the following pages are designed to help you; adjust the quantities suggested to suit the needs of your own children.

NOTES

All spoon measurements are level.

Ovens should be preheated to the temperature specified.

Freshly ground black pepper is intended where pepper is listed.

Fresh herbs are used unless otherwise stated. If unobtainable dried herbs can be substituted in cooked dishes but halve the quantities.

Eggs are U.S. grade large unless otherwise stated.

BREAKFASTS

A good breakfast sets your child up for the day ahead and builds up reserves of energy for play. Without proper nourishment in the morning, children are unable to cope with the stress of each day: they tire quickly and by mid-morning there is a noticeable falling-off in concentration.

Store-bought or home-made cereals, such as Munchy Crunch on page 10, make a good start to the day—avoid sugar coatings though and try to develop their tastes toward wholegrain rather than over-refined cereals. Cheesy Waffles (page 12), Banana and Bacon Kebabs and Cheese and Potato Patties (pages 8–9), all provide nourishment.

If your child won't eat so much early in the day, try serving Scotch Pancakes (below) or whole wheat bread with one of the spreads on pages 62–3. Alternatively try serving a nourishing drink such as Yognog (page 11) with a couple of whole wheat cookies or Picnic Squares (page 20) for a good start to any day.

SCOTCH PANCAKES

These are delicious served with Apricot Spread (page 62). If you prefer a savory breakfast, omit the honey and serve with cottage cheese and chives.

2 cups whole wheat
    flour
1 teaspoon cream of
    tartar
1/4 teaspoon baking
    soda
pinch of salt
1 egg

1 tablespoon corn oil
1 cup water
    (approximately)
1/2 cup skimmed milk
    powder
1 tablespoon honey
    (optional)

Makes 12–16
Preparation time:
20 minutes
Cooking time:
About 4 minutes
per batch
Freezing:
Recommended if
serving warm

1. Place the flour in a mixing bowl, sift in the cream of tartar, baking soda and salt and make a well in the center.
2. Add the egg, oil, half of the water, milk powder and honey, if using, and mix to a smooth batter. Beat in the remaining water, keeping the batter thick and smooth.
3. Heat a heavy-based frying pan or griddle and grease lightly. Drop in tablespoons of the batter and cook for about 2 minutes until the surface begins to bubble. Turn with a palette knife and cook for 1–2 minutes until the underside is golden brown.
4. Place the pancakes inside a clean folded dish cloth to keep moist until they are all cooked. Serve warm.

CHEESE AND POTATO PATTIES

These are really popular with most children and, because they are so quick and easy, with most moms! Delicious served with Carrot Salad (page 53) as an after-school snack, too.

1 lb potatoes, boiled and mashed
1 egg
3/4 cup grated sharp Cheddar cheese
2 scallions, chopped
1 tablespoon chopped parsley

1/2 cup fresh whole wheat breadcrumbs
salt and pepper to taste
whole wheat flour for coating
2 tablespoons salad oil for frying

Serves 4
Preparation time: 10 minutes, plus cooking potatoes
Cooking time: About 3 minutes per batch
Freezing: Recommended

1. Place all the ingredients in a bowl and beat together well. Leave to cool, then shape into 16 patties and coat with the flour.
2. Heat the oil in a non-stick pan and fry the patties in 2 batches for 1–2 minutes on each side until golden. Serve hot.

WHOLE WHEAT CHEESE TOASTIES

A quick snack which my children like for breakfast.

2 tomatoes, sliced
2 whole wheat or English muffins, halved and toasted

1/4 teaspoon dried oregano
1/2 cup grated sharp Cheddar cheese
salt and pepper to taste

Serves 2 or 4
Preparation time: 5 minutes
Cooking time: 2–3 minutes
Freezing: Not recommended

1. Place a few tomato slices on each muffin half and sprinkle with the oregano, salt and pepper and cheese.
2. Broil for 2–3 minutes, until brown and bubbling. Serve immediately.

BANANA AND BACON KEBABS

A delicious combination of flavors—and very quick to make. For young children, cut the bananas and bacon strips in half again, to make bite-size pieces.

2 small or medium bananas

4 strips bacon

1. Cut each banana into four pieces.
2. Stretch the bacon strips with a palette knife and cut in half. Wrap each half around a piece of banana and place on 2 metal skewers.
3. Broil for 3 minutes on each side. Remove the kebabs from their skewers and serve with whole wheat toast.

Serves 2 or 4 young children
Preparation time:
5 minutes
Cooking time:
6 minutes
Freezing:
Not recommended

FRUIT YOGURT

A delicious way to start the day, followed by whole wheat toast and Apricot Spread or Peanut and Celery Spread (pages 62–3).

⅓ cup halved
  strawberries
⅔ cup plain yogurt
1 teaspoon honey

1 banana, chopped
1 peach, pitted and
  chopped
1 oz green grapes, halved
  and seeded

Serves 3
Preparation time:
5 minutes
Freezing:
Not recommended

1. Place the strawberries in a bowl. Mix the yogurt with the honey and spoon over the strawberries. Add the remaining ingredients and mix thoroughly.
2. Divide the fruit yogurt between 3 individual bowls and serve immediately.

MUNCHY CRUNCH

A crisp granola that is delicious served with milk or yogurt, or just nibbled as it is. This quantity is enough for several days; stored in a screw-top jar it will keep for up to one month.

3 tablespoons sunflower
  oil
3 tablespoons honey

3 cups unsweetened
  muesli
1 oz dried banana chips,
  broken roughly

Makes 4½ cups
Preparation time:
15 minutes
Cooking time:
30–35 minutes
Freezing:
Not recommended

1. Place the oil and honey in a saucepan and heat gently until blended. Stir in the muesli and mix until well coated.
2. Turn the mixture into a large roasting pan and bake in a 350°F oven for 30–35 minutes, stirring occasionally so that it browns evenly.
3. Leave to cool, breaking up the lumps as it does so; if you prefer a finer consistency, work in a food processor or blender as desired. Stir in the banana chips.

VARIATION
Strawberry Crunch. Place 2 tablespoons yogurt in each individual bowl. Add ⅓ cup sliced strawberries to each, then sprinkle with Munchy Crunch.

YOGNOG

Ideal for a hurried breakfast because it is very nourishing. Hand them a Picnic Square (page 20) as they rush out of the door!

²/₃ cup plain yogurt　　　*1 egg*
¹/₂ cup milk　　　　　　*1 ripe banana*

Serves 2
Preparation time: 5 minutes
Freezing: Not recommended

1. Place all the ingredients in a blender or food processor and work together until smooth.
2. Pour into 2 glasses and serve.

CHEESY WAFFLES

This recipe can be made in advance and stored in the freezer for that morning when everyone is late and you have to produce a breakfast pronto! Just pop them in the toaster. If you do not have a waffle iron, buy some ready-made whole wheat waffles.

3/4 cup whole wheat flour
sifted with 1 teaspoon
baking powder
2 tablespoons grated
Parmesan cheese

1 tablespoon salad oil
1 egg, separated
1 cup milk

Makes 4
Preparation time:
10 minutes
Cooking time:
About 20 minutes
Freezing:
Recommended

1. Place the flour and Parmesan cheese in a bowl. Make a well in the center and add the oil, egg yolk and milk. Gradually incorporate the flour and beat until smooth.
2. Beat the egg white until fairly stiff, then fold carefully into the batter.
3. Spoon a quarter of the mixture into a heated and oiled non-stick waffle iron and cook for 2–3 minutes on each side, until crisp and golden. Keep warm while cooking the remaining batter.
4. Serve hot, with cottage cheese and tomatoes.

EGG BASKETS

3 slices whole wheat
bread, crusts removed
spreadable margarine
1 teaspoon salad oil

1 large tomato, skinned
and chopped
2 eggs
salt and pepper to taste

Serves 3
Preparation time:
5 minutes
Cooking time:
8–10 minutes
Freezing:
Not recommended

1. Roll the bread lightly with a rolling pin, so that it bends more easily. Spread one side of the bread with margarine, then lightly grease 3 muffin cups with margarine.
2. Press the bread, margarine side up, into the cups to form a basket shape. Bake in a 400°F oven for 8–10 minutes, until crisp.
3. Meanwhile, heat the oil in a small pan, add the tomato and cook for 1 minute.
4. Beat the eggs together with salt and pepper, add to the pan and cook, stirring constantly, until scrambled.
5. Place the bread baskets on 3 individual plates and divide the filling between them.

IDEAS FOR LUNCH BOXES

Packing healthy meals for children can be quite a problem—they invariably crave junk food. Here are recipes that are quick to prepare, easy to pack and transport, and taste good too.

Young children like individual packages: little boxes of raisins, pots of salad and small cartons of fruit juice. The salads are delicious packed into whole wheat pitta bread. Always include fresh fruit, and if your children look for something sweeter, dried fruit is a healthier alternative to candy.

CHEESE AND TOMATO SALAD

Rice or chopped vegetables can be added to this salad.

3/4 cup diced Cheddar cheese
1 celery stick, chopped
2 tomatoes, chopped
2 inch piece cucumber, chopped
2 scallions, chopped

FOR THE DRESSING:
1/4 cup cream cheese beaten with 1 tablespoon lemon juice
1 tablespoon salad oil
1 teaspoon cider vinegar
1/2 teaspoon tomato paste
salt and pepper to taste

Serves 3
Preparation time:
10 minutes
Freezing:
Not recommended

1. Mix all the dressing ingredients together in a bowl.
2. Add the salad ingredients and mix well until coated in the dressing. Pack in individual plastic containers.

CURRIED CHICKEN SALAD

If your children don't like curry, omit the curry powder and blend in 1 teaspoon tomato paste instead.

3 tablespoons mayonnaise
2 tablespoons plain yogurt
1/2 teaspoon curry powder
1/2 teaspoon honey
1 cup cubed cooked chicken

1/2 red pepper, cored, seeded and sliced thinly
2 pineapple slices, cut into pieces
2 scallions, sliced
1/4 cup whole wheat pasta shapes, cooked

Serves 2
Preparation time:
5 minutes
Freezing:
Not recommended

1. Mix the mayonnaise, yogurt, curry powder and honey together in a bowl.
2. Add the remaining ingredients and mix well until coated. Pack in individual rigid plastic containers.

TUNA AND TOMATO SALAD

This salad is also good with whole wheat pasta shapes instead of red kidney beans.

4 oz can tuna, drained
7 oz can red kidney beans,
*   drained*
2 tomatoes, chopped

1½ inch piece cucumber,
*   chopped*
1 tablespoon snipped
*   chives*
2 tablespoons French
*   dressing*

Serves 2–3
Preparation time:
5 minutes
Freezing:
Not recommended

1. Flake the tuna into a bowl. Add the beans, tomatoes, cucumber and chives, pour over the dressing and toss.
2. Spoon into individual rigid plastic containers.

CHEESE AND PINEAPPLE DIP WITH VEGETABLE STICKS

⅓ cup cream cheese
*   beaten with 1 table-*
*   spoon lemon juice*
2 tablespoons crushed
*   pineapple, drained*
1 tablespoon snipped
*   chives*
salt and pepper to taste

TO SERVE:
carrots
cucumber
celery
red pepper
cauliflower, divided into
*   florets*

Serves 1–2
Preparation time:
10 minutes
Freezing:
Not recommended

1. Mix all the ingredients together in a bowl.
2. Choose a colorful selection of vegetables from those listed and cut into sticks. Pack the dip and the sticks in individual yogurt pots or plastic containers.

DEVILED CHICKEN DRUMSTICKS

Wrap the ends of the drumsticks in foil to make them easier to hold. These can also be cooked on a barbecue.

4 chicken drumsticks
FOR THE BARBECUE
*   SAUCE:*
2 tablespoons Tomato
*   Sauce (page 37)*
2 tablespoons Spicy Fruit
*   Sauce (page 36)*

1 teaspoon soy sauce
*   (preferably Japanese)*
1 teaspoon Worcestershire
*   sauce*
1 teaspoon honey
¼ teaspoon mustard

1. Mix all the sauce ingredients together.
2. Make 2 deep cuts on each drumstick and brush all over with the sauce.
3. Place on a piece of foil and broil for about 15 minutes, turning frequently and basting with the remaining sauce, until they are cooked through. Serve hot or cold.

Serves 2
Preparation time:
5 minutes
Cooking time:
About 15 minutes
Freezing:
Not recommended

CHEESE AND CORN PASTIES

Freeze any extra pasties for future. The result will be better if you freeze them uncooked, then cook from frozen for 30 minutes when needed.

2 tablespoons salad oil
1 onion, chopped
2 celery sticks, chopped
1 clove garlic, crushed
1 tablespoon whole wheat
  flour
1/3 cup milk
3/4 cup grated Edam
  cheese
1/2 cup whole kernel corn

2 tablespoons chopped
  parsley
1 teaspoon Dijon
  mustard
3/4 lb frozen whole wheat
  puff pastry, thawed
2 teaspoons sesame
  seeds
salt and pepper to taste

Makes 6
Preparation time:
35 minutes
Cooking time:
20 minutes
Freezing:
Recommended, at end of stage 5

1. Heat the oil in a pan, add the onion, celery and garlic and fry gently until softened.
2. Stir in the flour, then gradually blend in the milk. Bring to the boil, stirring constantly, and cook for 3 minutes, until thickened.
3. Stir in the cheese, corn, parsley, mustard, and salt and pepper and leave to cool.
4. Meanwhile, roll the pastry out thinly on a floured surface and cut into eight 6 inch circles.
5. Divide the mixture between the circles, heaping it in the center. Moisten the edge with water, fold in half to make a semi-circle and pinch the edges together firmly.
6. Place on a baking sheet, brush with water and sprinkle with sesame seeds. Make a hole in each one.
7. Bake in a 425°F oven for 20 minutes. Cool on the baking sheet.

SALAD SANDWICHES

This is one of our favorite picnic foods—long whole wheat bread or rolls, split and filled to bursting with tuna and salad. Remember the napkins!

1 long whole wheat
  roll
3 tablespoons French
  dressing
2 tomatoes, sliced

1 1/2 inch piece cucumber,
  sliced
few lettuce leaves
4 oz can tuna, drained

1. Split the roll along one side without cutting right through, then open out so that it lies flat.
2. Sprinkle the French dressing all over the inside of the bread. Cover with the tomatoes, cucumber, lettuce and tuna, then close together. Cut in half.
3. Wrap each piece in foil, place a board on top and weigh down for 1 hour—this is not essential, but it makes them easier to eat!

Makes 2
Preparation time:
10 minutes
Freezing:
Not recommended

PICNIC SQUARES

These are as good as, or better than, a bowl of cereal for an instant breakfast, or make part of a healthy lunch. Although the crunchiness is very popular, you may prefer to leave out the nuts for young children.

*3 tablespoons malt
   extract
2 tablespoons honey
1/2 cup sunflower oil
1 cup jumbo oats*

*1 cup rolled oats
1/4 cup sunflower seeds
1/4 cup peanuts, chopped
   finely*

Makes 24
Preparation time:
10 minutes
Cooking time:
25–30 minutes
Freezing:
Recommended

1. Place the malt, honey and oil in a pan and heat gently until combined. Remove from the heat, add the remaining ingredients and mix thoroughly.
2. Press into a greased 12 × 8 inch jelly roll pan and smooth the top with a palette knife.
3. Bake in a 350°F oven for 25–30 minutes.
4. Cool in the pan for 2 minutes, then cut into squares. Cool completely before removing from the pan.

FRUITY FINGERS

1¾ cups whole wheat
   flour
1 teaspoon each ground
   mixed spice and
   cinnamon
¾ cup margarine
⅔ cup dark brown sugar,
   packed
2 tablespoons malt
   extract

4 eggs
1½ cups currants
1½ cups golden raisins
1¼ cups raisins
1 tablespoon orange
   juice
3 tablespoons chopped
   walnuts

1. Grease and line an 11 × 7 inch baking pan.
2. Place the flour in a bowl and sift in the spices.
3. Cream the margarine with the sugar and malt extract until fluffy. Beat in the eggs one at a time, adding a tablespoon of flour with all but the first. Fold in the remaining flour with the fruits and orange juice.
4. Turn the mixture into the prepared pan, smooth the surface and sprinkle with the walnuts.
5. Bake in a 325°F oven for 1–1¼ hours, until a skewer pierced through the center comes out clean.
6. Cool on a rack, then cut into fingers.

Makes 20
Preparation time:
30 minutes
Cooking time:
1–1¼ hours
Freezing:
Recommended

HAMBURGERS

Bulgur wheat swells to about 4 times its dry size, bulking out the meat and making a healthier burger.

*⅓ cup bulgur wheat,
  soaked in boiling water
  for 20 minutes
½ lb ground beef
1 small carrot, grated
½ onion, chopped finely
1 clove garlic*

*1 tablespoon soy sauce
  (preferably Japanese)
1 teaspoon Worcestershire
  sauce
salt and pepper to taste
salad oil for brushing*

**Makes 4
Preparation time:**
15 minutes, plus
soaking time
Cooking time:
8 minutes
Freezing:
Recommended, at
end of stage 1

1. Drain the bulgur wheat in a sieve, pressing out the water. Turn into a bowl and mix with the remaining ingredients, using your hands. Form into 4 burgers.
2. Brush lightly with oil and broil for about 4 minutes on each side.
3. Serve with salad or in whole wheat buns, with Spicy Fruit Sauce (page 36) or Tomato Sauce (page 37).

MILLIGETTI

Millet is used to cut down on the quantity of meat needed in this recipe—its texture is ideal.

*1 tablespoon salad oil
1 onion, chopped
1 clove garlic, crushed
½ lb ground beef
1 tablespoon all-purpose
  flour
⅓ cup millet or bulgur
  wheat*

*14 oz can tomatoes
1 tablespoon tomato
  paste
1 tablespoon soy sauce
  (preferably Japanese)
1¼ cups vegetable stock
salt and pepper to taste
grated cheese to serve*

**Serves 4
Preparation time:**
15 minutes
Cooking time:
35 minutes
Freezing:
Recommended

1. Heat the oil in a saucepan, add the onion and fry until softened. Add the garlic and beef and cook, stirring so that the meat is broken up as it seals. Remove from the heat, drain off any fat, then stir in the flour.
2. Add the remaining ingredients, bring to the boil, then cover and simmer for 35 minutes, until cooked.
3. Serve with cheese and whole wheat spaghetti.

TUNA CASSEROLE

This dish is also very good made with cooked smoked
haddock or chicken.

2 carrots, sliced
2 celery sticks, sliced
1 cup frozen peas
1 1/2 cups dried whole
*   wheat pasta*
2 tablespoons salad oil
1 onion, chopped
2 tablespoons whole
*   wheat flour*

1 1/4 cups milk
*   (approximately)*
7 oz can tuna, drained
*   and flaked*
1 cup grated Cheddar
*   cheese*
3 tablespoons whole
*   wheat breadcrumbs*

Serves 4
Preparation time:
15 minutes
Cooking time:
20 minutes
Freezing:
Recommended

1. Place the carrots and celery in a pan, cover with
cold water and bring to the boil. Cover and cook for
15 minutes, adding the peas for the last 5 minutes.
Drain, reserving the liquid, and set aside. Meanwhile,
cook the pasta according to package instructions; drain
and set aside.
2. Heat the oil in a pan, add the onion and cook until
softened. Remove from the heat and stir in the flour.
3. Make up the reserved liquid to 2 cups with the milk.
Gradually add to the pan, stirring constantly until
blended. Bring to the boil and cook for 3 minutes, until
thickened.
4. Add the vegetables, pasta, tuna and half of the cheese.
Turn into a shallow ovenproof dish and sprinkle with
the remaining cheese and breadcrumbs.
5. Broil for 3–4 minutes, until golden brown and
bubbling. Serve immediately.

SCONE PIZZA

2 cups whole wheat flour
*   sifted with 3 teaspoons*
*   baking powder*
1/2 teaspoon salt
1/2 teaspoon dried mixed
*   herbs*
1/4 cup margarine
1/2 cup skimmed milk
FOR THE TOPPING:
1 tablespoon salad oil
1 onion, chopped

14 oz can tomatoes,
*   drained and chopped*
1/2 teaspoon dried
*   oregano*
1 tablespoon tomato
*   paste*
4 oz Mozzarella cheese,
*   sliced*
4 black olives, halved and
*   pitted*
salt and pepper to taste

1. Place the flour, salt and herbs in a mixing bowl and rub in the margarine until the mixture resembles breadcrumbs. Add the milk and mix to a soft dough.
2. Turn onto a floured surface and knead lightly, then roll out to a 10 inch circle. Place on a floured baking sheet and bake in a 425°F oven for 10 minutes, until risen and firm.
3. Meanwhile, make the topping. Heat the oil in a pan, add the onion and fry until softened. Add the tomatoes, oregano, and salt and pepper and cook for 3 minutes.
4. Spread the tomato paste over the cooked scone, then spoon the tomato mixture over the top, spreading to the edge. Arrange the Mozzarella on top and finish with the olives.
5. Return to the oven for about 5 minutes, until the cheese has melted. Serve immediately.

Serves 4
Preparation time:
20 minutes
Cooking time:
About 15 minutes
Freezing:
Recommended

HAM MOUSSE

2 tablespoons honey
1 teaspoon dry mustard
2 eggs, beaten
1/4 cup white wine vinegar
1 tablespoon gelatin,
    soaked in 3 table-
    spoons cold water

1 1/4 cups cream cheese
    beaten with 1/3 cup
    lemon juice
1 1/2 cups cubed ham
salt and pepper to taste

Serves 6
Preparation time:
15 minutes
Setting time:
1 hour
Freezing:
Recommended

1. Mix the honey, mustard, and salt and pepper together until blended. Add the eggs and vinegar and heat gently, stirring constantly, until thickened.
2. Add the gelatin and stir until dissolved, then leave to cool.
3. Stir in the cream cheese mixture and ham. Turn into 6 lightly oiled ramekins and leave to set. Serve with whole wheat toast and raw carrot sticks or tomatoes.

SPICY SAUSAGES

Sausages will always be a favorite with children. Try these healthy home-made ones.

2 cups whole wheat
    breadcrumbs
1/4 cup water
1/2 lb ground beef
1 small onion, chopped
    finely
1 clove garlic, crushed
1 egg yolk

2 tablespoons tomato
    paste
1 teaspoon paprika
1 teaspoon ground
    coriander
whole wheat flour for
    coating
salt and pepper to taste

Serves 4–6
Preparation time:
20 minutes
Cooking time:
8–10 minutes
Freezing:
Recommended

1. Place the breadcrumbs in a bowl, pour over the water and mix together. Add the remaining ingredients and mix thoroughly with your hand.
2. Divide the mixture into 12 portions and, with dampened hands, roll each portion into a 4½ inch long thin sausage shape, then roll in the flour to coat evenly.
3. Broil for 8–10 minutes, turning occasionally. Serve with Tomato Sauce (page 37), mashed potato and a vegetable accompaniment, or in whole wheat pitta bread with salad.

TOMATO AND POTATO BAKE

I find ground beef dishes are always a favorite; here I use Milligetti as the base. It can, of course, be made in one large dish, but individual ones look more appealing.

1 quantity Milligetti
(page 22)
4 tomatoes, sliced
¼ cup Tomato Sauce
(page 37)

1 lb potatoes, boiled and
sliced
salad oil for brushing

Serves 4
Preparation time:
10 minutes, plus making Milligetti and cooking potatoes
Cooking time:
30 minutes
Freezing:
Not recommended

1. Divide the Milligetti between 4 individual ovenproof dishes and arrange the tomato slices on top.
2. Spread the tomato sauce over each one, then arrange the potatoes in overlapping slices on top.
3. Brush lightly with oil and cook in a 400°F oven for 30 minutes, until lightly browned. Serve hot.

MEATY HOLLOWS

2¼ lb potatoes, peeled
⅓ cup milk
1 quantity Milligetti
(page 22)

1 cup grated Cheddar
cheese
salt and pepper to taste

Serves 6
Preparation time:
35 minutes, plus making Milligetti
Cooking time:
15 minutes
Freezing:
Recommended

1. Boil the potatoes in salted water for about 15 minutes until cooked. Drain thoroughly, mash, then move to one side of the pan and pour in the milk. Heat slightly, then beat thoroughly with a wooden spoon until white and fluffy. Add salt and pepper and beat again.
2. Cool slightly, then place half of the mixture in a piping bag fitted with a large fluted tip and pipe a border around 3 greased individual ovenproof dishes. Repeat with the remaining potato on 3 more dishes.
3. Spoon the heated milligetti into each hollow and sprinkle with the cheese.
4. Bake in a 400°F oven for 15 minutes, until brown and bubbling. Serve hot.

TIKKA KEBABS

These kebabs have a slightly spicy flavor. They can also be barbecued.

1 tablespoon salad oil
1 clove garlic
1 teaspoon tandoori spice mix
¼ cup plain yogurt
1 tablespoon lemon juice
¾ lb lean lamb, cut into 1 inch cubes
1 red pepper, cored, seeded and cut into squares

2 small onions, each cut into 8 pieces
FOR THE FRIED RICE:
1 tablespoon salad oil
1 onion, chopped
12 oz cooked brown rice
7 oz can whole kernel corn, drained
1 tablespoon chopped parsley

Serves 4
Preparation time: 15 minutes, plus cooking rice
Cooking time: 8 minutes
Freezing: Not recommended

1. Mix together the oil, garlic, spice, yogurt and lemon juice. Add the meat and stir until well coated.
2. Thread alternate pieces of lamb, red pepper and onion onto 4 large or 8 small skewers. Broil for 8 minutes, turning frequently.
3. Meanwhile, make the fried rice: heat the oil in a non-stick pan, add the onion and fry until softened. Add the remaining ingredients and stir constantly until heated through.
4. Serve the kebabs with the rice.

MINTY MEAT BALLS

Children love meat balls. By adding fiber to them in the form of bulgur wheat and whole wheat breadcrumbs you can serve a healthy meal.

3 tablespoons bulgur wheat, soaked in boiling water for 20 minutes
1 cup whole wheat breadcrumbs
½ lb ground lamb
3 tablespoons chopped mint
1 egg

1 clove garlic, crushed
1 onion, chopped finely
1 teaspoon Worcestershire sauce
salt and pepper to taste
whole wheat flour for coating
2 tablespoons salad oil for frying

1. Drain the bulgur wheat in a sieve, pressing out as much water as possible. Turn into a bowl and stir in the breadcrumbs.

2. Add the remaining ingredients and mix together by hand until well blended. Form into small balls, with dampened hands, then coat in flour.

3. Heat the oil in a non-stick frying pan and fry the meat balls for 8–10 minutes, shaking the pan occasionally to turn them.

4. Drain on paper towels and serve with Tomato Sauce (page 37), peas and whole wheat pasta shapes.

Serves 4
Preparation time:
30 minutes, plus soaking time
Cooking time:
8–10 minutes
Freezing:
Recommended

CHUNKY CHICKEN RICE

Small chicken joints could be used instead of cooked chicken. Add to the rice with the apple juice and stock.

2 tablespoons salad oil
1 large onion, chopped
1 clove garlic, crushed
2 celery sticks, chopped
2/3 cup brown rice
2/3 cup apple juice
1 1/4 cups chicken stock or
water

3/4 cup tomato sauce
1 cup frozen peas
1 1/2 cups chopped cooked
chicken
2 tablespoons chopped
parsley
salt and pepper to taste

Serves 4
Preparation time:
25 minutes
Cooking time:
45 minutes
Freezing:
Recommended

1. Heat the oil in a large flameproof casserole, add the onion, garlic and celery and fry gently for about 10 minutes, stirring occasionally.
2. Add the rice and stir until coated with oil, then fry for 1 minute. Add the apple juice, stock or water, and salt and pepper and bring to the boil. Cover and cook in a 375°F oven for 30 minutes.
3. Add the tomato sauce, peas and chicken, stir thoroughly and return to the oven for 15 minutes.
4. Stir in the parsley and serve with a salad such as Apple Coleslaw (page 52).

CHICKEN AND CORN CREPES

The batter makes 10–12 crepes and the filling is enough to fill 8 of them. Freeze the extra crepes, for occasions when you need to produce a quick dish.

FOR THE BATTER:
1 cup whole wheat
flour
1 egg
1 1/4 cups milk
1 tablespoon salad oil
FOR THE FILLING:
1 tablespoon salad oil
1 onion, chopped
1/4 cup whole wheat
flour
1 1/4 cups milk

1 1/4 cups diced cooked
chicken
7 oz can whole kernel
corn, drained
1 tablespoon chopped
parsley
salt and pepper to
taste
TO FINISH:
3/4 cup grated Cheddar
cheese

1. Place the batter ingredients in a food processor or blender and work together for 30 seconds. Leave to stand for 15 minutes.

2. Meanwhile, make the filling: heat the oil in a pan, add the onion and cook until softened. Remove from the heat and stir in the flour, then gradually add the milk, stirring until blended. Bring back to the boil, stirring constantly, and cook for 3 minutes, until thickened. Add the remaining ingredients.

3. Heat a 6 inch omelet pan and add a few drops of oil. Pour in 1 tablespoon of the batter and tilt the pan to coat the bottom evenly. Cook until the underside is brown, then turn and cook for 10 seconds. Turn onto a warmed plate.

4. Repeat with the remaining batter, making 10–12 crepes. Stack, interleaved with waxed paper, as they are cooked.

5. Divide the filling between 8 of the crepes, roll up and place in a shallow ovenproof dish. Sprinkle with the cheese and cook in a 375°F oven for 15 minutes. Serve immediately, with a salad.

Serves 4
Preparation time: 35 minutes
Cooking time: 15 minutes
Freezing: Recommended

FISH CAKES

1 lb potatoes, boiled and mashed	*2 tablespoons snipped chives*
¾ lb cod, haddock or whiting, cooked and flaked	*1 cup whole wheat breadcrumbs*
1 tablespoon tomato paste	*salt and pepper to taste*
	salad oil for frying

Serves 4–6
Preparation time:
25 minutes
Cooking time:
10 minutes
Freezing:
Recommended

1. Mix together the potatoes, fish, tomato paste, chives, and salt and pepper. Shape into 24 small flat patties, then coat with the breadcrumbs.
2. Heat a little oil in a non-stick frying pan and fry the fish cakes in 2 batches for 5 minutes, turning once.
3. Drain well on paper towels. Serve immediately, with Tomato Sauce (page 37) and peas or a salad.

FISH IN THE RED SEA

Choose the fillets carefully—little ones look best.

2 whiting fillets, skinned	*2 teaspoons all-purpose flour*
1 bay leaf	*½ clove garlic, crushed*
1 parsley sprig	*8 oz can tomatoes*
1 lemon slice	*salt and pepper to taste*
⅔ cup water	*TO GARNISH:*
FOR THE SAUCE:	*4 slices cucumber*
2 teaspoons salad oil	*1 stuffed olive, sliced*
½ onion, chopped	

Serves 1 or 2
Preparation time:
10 minutes
Cooking time:
About 15 minutes
Freezing:
Not recommended

1. Place the fish in an ovenproof dish with the bay leaf, parsley and lemon slice. Pour over the water, sprinkle with salt and pepper and cover with foil.
2. Cook in a 350°F oven for about 15 minutes, until the fish looks opaque.
3. Meanwhile, make the sauce. Heat the oil in a pan, add the onion and fry until softened. Stir in the flour and garlic, then gradually add the tomatoes with their juice, and salt and pepper. Cover and simmer for 10 minutes. Cool slightly, then puree in a food processor or blender.
4. Skin the fillets and place on 1 or 2 warmed individual plates. Cut and arrange the cucumber to look like a tail, head and gills and position the olive slices for eyes.
5. Pour the tomato sauce around each fish to serve.

EGGHEADS

Eggs stuffed with tuna filling then decorated with salad will appeal to most small children. Any extra tuna filling can be refrigerated and used in sandwiches.

2 *hard-boiled eggs*	*TO FINISH:*
4 *oz can tuna, drained*	2 *stuffed olives*
½ *cup cream cheese*	4 *tiny sour gherkins*
beaten with 2 table-	*few curly endive leaves*
spoons lemon juice	4 *cherry tomatoes, halved*
2 *teaspoons Tomato*	¼ *cucumber, sliced*
Sauce (opposite)	4 *slices carrot*
salt and pepper to taste	

Serves 4
Preparation time:
15 minutes
Freezing:
Not recommended

1. Cut the eggs in half lengthways, remove the yolks and rub through a sieve.
2. Mash the tuna, then mix with the cream cheese mixture, egg yolks, tomato sauce, and salt and pepper.
3. Divide the mixture between the egg whites and shape into mounds with a palette knife.
4. Cut and arrange the olives and gherkins on each egg to resemble a face, and place on individual plates.
5. Arrange the curly endive around the top of each egg to resemble hair, tomatoes to make ears, cucumber slices for the shirt and carrot pieces for bow ties.

SPICY FRUIT SAUCE

⅓ *cup pitted prunes*	½ *cup tomato juice*
⅔ *cup water*	1 *tablespoon soy sauce*
1 *tablespoon salad oil*	*(preferably Japanese)*
1 *onion, chopped*	2 *tablespoons cider*
1 *clove garlic, crushed*	*vinegar*
¼ *teaspoon each ground*	*salt and pepper to taste*
cloves, cumin, ginger	
and grated nutmeg	

Makes 1¼ cups
Preparation time:
40 minutes
Freezing:
Recommended

1. Use the prunes and water to make a prune puree following the instructions for Prune Spread on page 62.
2. Heat the oil in a pan, add the onion and fry until softened. Add the garlic and spices and fry for 1 minute.
3. Place in a food processor or blender, add all the other ingredients and work until smooth.
4. Pour into a clean bottle and store in the refrigerator for up to 1 month.

TOMATO SAUCE

If you do not use tomato sauce very often, freeze half of this quantity for future use.

2 tablespoons olive oil
2 cloves garlic, crushed
3 tablespoons whole wheat flour
1 tablespoon tomato paste
1 cup apple juice
1 1/4 cups tomato sauce

1/4 teaspoon dried oregano
1 teaspoon Worcestershire sauce
1 tablespoon wine vinegar
salt and pepper to taste

1. Heat the oil in a pan, add the garlic and fry for 2 minutes. Remove from the heat and stir in the flour and tomato puree.
2. Blend the apple juice, return to the heat, bring to the boil and cook for 3 minutes, until thickened.
3. Add the remaining ingredients, mix together thoroughly and leave to cool.
4. Pour into a clean bottle and store in the refrigerator for up to 8 days.

Makes 2 1/4 cups
Preparation time: 10 minutes
Cooking time: 5 minutes
Freezing: Recommended

DESERTS

KNICKERBOCKER GLORY

A healthy concoction the kids are bound to love. Add a scoop of Strawberry Ice Cream (page 45) to each portion if you have some in the freezer.

2/3 cup raspberries
1 cup curd cheese or
farmer's cheese
2 tablespoons honey
1 1/4 cups sliced
strawberries

2 bananas, sliced
1 1/4 cups sour cream
4 strawberries, sliced, to
decorate

Serves 4
Preparation time:
15 minutes
Freezing:
Not recommended

1. Press the raspberries through a sieve to make a puree. Gradually add cheese and honey and mix until smooth.
2. Place a few strawberry and banana slices in 4 tall glasses, place a spoonful of the raspberry mixture on top, then pour over a spoonful of sour cream.
3. Repeat the layers twice more, finishing with sour cream. Decorate with sliced strawberries to serve.

STRAWBERRY SALAD

A quick and delicious way of introducing fresh fruit into the diet. It looks very pretty and tastes wonderful.

3 oranges
1 1/2 cups halved
strawberries

1 tablespoon honey
sour cream or Greek
yogurt to serve

Serves 4
Preparation time:
10 minutes
Freezing:
Not recommended

1. Peel and segment the oranges, discarding all pith and pits, and place in a bowl with any juice.
2. Add the strawberries and honey, and mix together so that all the fruit is coated. Chill thoroughly.
3. Spoon into 4 individual dishes and serve with sour cream or Greek yogurt.

Illustrated bottom
right: Frothy Fool
(page 40)

FROTHY FOOL

Any soft fruit in season can be used for this fool. Greek strained yogurt gives the best results, but other types can be substituted.

Serves 6
Preparation time:
10 minutes
Cooking time:
5 minutes
Freezing:
Not recommended

Illustrated on
page 39

3 cups blackberries
2 tablespoons honey

1 cup Greek strained
   yogurt
1 egg white

1. Place the blackberries and honey in a pan and simmer gently for 5 minutes, until softened.
2. Leave to cool, then strain off any excess liquid. Puree the blackberries in a food processor or blender, then sieve to remove pits. Mix with the yogurt.
3. Beat the egg white until stiff, then fold into the fruit mixture. Serve immediately in individual dishes.

FRUIT BOATS

These little boats are especially attractive to younger children. If you are short of time, the gelatin would still look very pretty served in small dishes.

Makes 8
Preparation time:
20 minutes
Setting time:
1 hour
Freezing:
Not recommended

2 large oranges
1/3 cup orange juice
   (approximately)
1 sachet gelatin, soaked
   in 2 tablespoons cold
   water

2 teaspoons honey
1/4 cup raspberries
1/2 banana, sliced
TO FINISH:
1 sheet rice paper
8 cocktail sticks

1. Cut the oranges in half crossways, then squeeze to extract the juice. Strain into a measuring pitcher and make up to 1 cup with the orange juice.
2. Using a small spoon, scrape out and discard all the membrane and pith from the orange halves, being careful not to pierce the skins.
3. Arrange the shells close together on a baking sheet.
4. Heat the gelatin gently until dissolved, then add to the orange juice with the honey.
5. Stir in the raspberries and banana, cool slightly, then pour into the orange skins. Chill for 1 hour, until set.
6. When firm, cut in half with a sharp knife.
7. Cut the rice paper into triangles, spear with a cocktail stick and arrange on each 'boat' to resemble a sail.

WATERMELON BOATS

Fresh fruit is a healthy way to finish off a meal. It is much more enticing if served in this way.

4 thin slices watermelon
3 oranges, peeled and
* segmented*

2 kiwi fruit, peeled and
* sliced*
4 mint sprigs

1. Remove the pits from the watermelon slices, cut off the skin and lay each slice on its side on 4 individual plates.
2. Arrange the orange segments overlapping each other to represent a sail.
3. Halve the kiwi fruit slices and arrange under the melon to represent the sea. Place a 'flag' of mint on top of each 'sail'.

Serves 4
Preparation time:
15 minutes
Freezing:
Not recommended

ORANGE CREPES

If you have crepes in the freezer, take out the number you need and adjust the amount of the filling.

FOR THE BATTER:
1 cup whole wheat flour
1 egg
1¼ cups milk
1 tablespoon salad oil
FOR THE FILLING:
2 oranges

1 cup cream cheese
  beaten with ¼ cup
  lemon juice
1 tablespoon honey
TO FINISH:
2 tablespoon sugar-free
  apricot jam, warmed

Serves 5–6
Preparation time:
15 minutes, plus
making crepes
Cooking time:
15 minutes
Freezing:
Recommended
for crepes only

1. Make the batter and cook 10–12 crepes as for Chicken and Corn Crepes (page 32).
2. Grate the zest of 1 orange finely and mix with the cream cheese mixture and honey.
3. Peel the skin and pith from both oranges and cut into segments; reserve a few segments for decoration.
4. Spread a spoonful of filling on each crepe, place a few orange segments on top and roll up. Arrange on a heatproof dish and brush with a little apricot jam.
5. Bake in a 375°F oven for 15 minutes. Top with the reserved orange segments.

RASPBERRY CRUMBLE

This dessert is so scrumptious that few would believe it is so easily made. It is a favorite in my household during the raspberry season. Delicious by itself, but some might like a topping of sour cream.

*1 1/2 cups whole wheat
  flour*
1/3 cup margarine
*1/4 cup dark brown sugar,
  packed*

*1/4 cup chopped filberts
  (optional)*
*1/2 lb dessert apples,
  cored*
1 cup raspberries
2 tablespoons honey

1. Place the flour in a bowl and rub in the margarine until the mixture resembles breadcrumbs, then mix in the sugar and nuts.
2. Slice the apples thinly and mix with the raspberries. Arrange in a 1 quart dish and drizzle over the honey.
3. Sprinkle the crumb mixture over the top to cover the fruit completely and press down lightly.
4. Bake in a 350°F oven for 45 minutes, until golden. Serve hot.

Serves 4
Preparation time:
20 minutes
Cooking time:
45 minutes
Freezing:
Recommended at end of stage 3

MINT CHIP ICE CREAM

You could use chocolate chips instead of the carob.

3 egg yolks
1/3 cup honey
1 1/4 cups milk
1 tablespoon gelatin,
soaked in 3
tablespoons cold
water

1 teaspoon peppermint
extract
15 oz can evaporated
milk, chilled
3 oz unsweetened carob
bar, chopped

Serves 6–8
Preparation time:
30 minutes
Freezing time:
4 hours

1. Mix the egg yolks and honey together in a heatproof bowl until blended.
2. Bring the milk almost to the boil in a heavy-based pan, pour onto the egg yolk mixture and blend well. Return to the pan and heat gently, stirring, until slightly thickened.
3. Add the gelatin and stir until dissolved. Cool slightly, then add the peppermint extract and leave until just beginning to set.
4. Beat the evaporated milk until thick, then beat into the mint custard. Fold in the carob chips. Turn into a rigid freezerproof container, cover, seal and freeze for 4 hours, until firm.
5. Transfer to the refrigerator 20 minutes before serving to soften. Scoop into chilled dishes to serve.

ORANGE AND HONEY ICE CREAM

2 oranges
2 egg yolks
1/4 cup honey

1 cup Greek strained
yogurt
2/3 cup heavy cream,
whipped

Serves 6
Preparation time:
20 minutes
Freezing time:
3–4 hours

1. Finely grate the rind of the oranges and mix with the egg yolks and honey. Squeeze the oranges and add the juice to the egg yolk mixture.
2. Pour into a double boiler or heavy-based pan and heat gently, stirring constantly, until thickened. Leave to cool.
3. Fold the orange custard into the yogurt, then beat into the cream. Turn into a rigid freezerproof container, cover, seal and freeze for 3–4 hours, until firm.
4. Leave at room temperature for 15 minutes to soften before serving. Scoop into chilled dishes to serve.

STRAWBERRY ICE CREAM

2 cups strawberries
1 cup Greek strained
yogurt

2 egg whites
¼ cup honey

1. Puree the strawberries in a food processor or blender, then sieve to remove the pits. Mix the puree with the yogurt until smooth.
2. Beat the egg whites until stiff, then beat in the honey. Fold into the strawberry mixture.
3. Turn into a rigid freezerproof container, cover, seal and freeze for 4 hours, until firm.
4. Transfer to the refrigerator 20 minutes before serving to soften. Scoop into chilled dishes to serve.

Serves 6
Preparation time:
15 minutes
Freezing time:
4 hours

SPICY APPLE PIES

These are delicious served warm with sour cream. They are also good cold, and are useful for lunch boxes.

3/4 lb dessert apples, peeled, cored and sliced
2 tablespoons apple juice
1 teaspoon ground cinnamon
2 tablespoons sultanas

FOR THE PASTRY:
1 1/2 cups whole wheat flour
1/3 cup margarine
2 tablespoons ice water
milk to glaze
1 tablespoon sesame seeds

Makes about 10
Preparation time:
50 minutes
Cooking time:
15–20 minutes
Freezing:
Recommended

1. Place the apples, apple juice and cinnamon in a saucepan, cover and simmer gently for 15 minutes, stirring occasionally. Add the sultanas and leave to cool, with the lid on.
2. Meanwhile make the pastry: place the flour in a bowl and rub in the margarine until the mixture resembles breadcrumbs. Add enough water to mix to a firm dough, then turn onto a lightly floured surface and knead lightly. Chill for 15 minutes.
3. Roll out the pastry thinly on a floured surface. Cut out about ten 3 inch and ten 2 inch circles.
4. Use the larger circles to line 10 muffin cups. Place a spoonful of the apple mixture in each. Dampen the edge and top with the remaining circles.
5. Press the edges to seal, make a hole in the center and brush with milk. Sprinkle with the sesame seeds.
6. Bake in a 400°F oven for 15–20 minutes, until golden. Serve warm or cold.

RASPBERRY ROLL

My children are always asking for chocolate desserts. Because I want them to eat more healthily, I use carob powder, though you could use cocoa powder.

3 eggs
1/3 cup dark brown sugar, packed
3/4 cup whole wheat flour
3 tablespoons carob powder, sifted
1 tablespoon superfine sugar

FOR THE FILLING:
1 cup curd cheese or farmer's cheese
2 tablespoons honey
1/2 cup raspberries, crushed

1. Grease and line a 12 × 8 inch jelly roll pan, then grease the paper.
2. Beat the eggs and sugar together for 10 minutes or until thick and mousse-like, using an electric beater.
3. Carefully fold in the flour and carob powder with a metal spoon, then turn into the prepared pan.
4. Bake in a 400°F oven for 8–10 minutes, until the sponge cake springs back when pressed in the center.
5. Wring out a clean dish cloth in hot water, lay it on a work surface, place a sheet of waxed paper on top and sprinkle with the superfine sugar.
6. Turn the sponge cake out onto the paper, carefully peel off the lining paper and trim off the crisp edges on the long sides.
7. Roll up the sponge cake with the sugared paper inside, remove the cloth, then place on a rack with the join underneath, to cool.
8. Mix the curd cheese or farmer's cheese with the honey and raspberries.
9. Unroll the sponge cake and remove the paper. Spread with the filling and roll up again. Cut into slices to serve.

Serves 6–8
Preparation time:
30 minutes
Cooking time:
8–10 minutes
Freezing:
Not recommended

AFTER-SCHOOL SNACKS

This chapter is largely aimed at children under school age who have had a more substantial meal at lunchtime. The recipes are mainly suitable to serve just before bedtime as a supper.

Some of the recipes have a novelty theme to appeal to an age group that is often difficult to please. For the same reason, it is better to make helpings small: give second helpings rather than overfilling the plates to begin with.

Also included here are a few snack ideas for the invariably 'starving' child arriving home from school. Popcorn, Cheese and Tomato Straws and Pinwheels (pages 64–5) are delicious alternatives to potato chips or candy. Make a batch of whole wheat scones (page 62) and freeze them—they take little time to thaw and can be removed individually from the freezer. Your children will find them irresistible served with the home-made spreads (pages 62–3).

NOVELTY SANDWICHES

2 hard-boiled eggs, chopped finely	6 slices whole wheat bread
¼ cup curd cheese or farmer's cheese	TO FINISH: radishes
2 tablespoons mayonnaise	carrots
1 carton cress or alfalfa sprouts	cucumber slices and cubes

Serves 3–4
Preparation time:
20 minutes
Freezing:
Not recommended

1. Mix the eggs, cheese, mayonnaise and cress together with a fork until smooth and use to make 3 rounds of sandwiches.
2. Remove the crusts and cut each sandwich into 4 squares. Set aside 6 squares for the 'trains'.
3. For the 'sandwich sea', cut each of the remaining squares into 4 triangles, and arrange on a plate.
4. To make the radish 'boats', cut the radishes in half lengthways. Using a potato peeler, peel off a few thin slices of carrot, spear with a cocktail stick and stick into the radish base to make 'sails'.
5. Arrange cucumber slices around the sandwiches and place the radish boats on the 'sea'.
6. For the 'trains', cut 2 of the reserved squares in half to make 4 'trucks'. Use the other 4 squares to make 2 'engines'. To finish, cut a carrot 'funnel', radish 'buffers', carrot 'wheels' and use diced cucumber to pile on the 'trucks' to resemble cargo. Arrange each 'train' on a layer of cucumber slices.

VIKING SHIPS

If sardines are not popular in your household, use tuna
or hard-boiled eggs instead.

*4 oz can sardines in oil,
   drained*
*½ cup cream cheese
   beaten with 2 table-
   spoons lemon juice*
*1 tablespoon tomato
   paste*

*6 small whole wheat rolls,
   halved*
salt and pepper to taste
TO FINISH:
24 radishes, sliced
3 tomatoes, quartered
12 cocktail sticks
parsley sprigs

Makes 12
Preparation time:
15 minutes
Freezing:
Not recommended

1. Place the sardines in a bowl and mash with a fork.
Add the cream cheese mixture, tomato paste, and salt
and pepper and mix thoroughly. Divide between the
rolls. Arrange the radish slices around the edges.
2. Cut the tomatoes into quarters, then scoop out and
discard the centers. Place a cocktail stick in each tomato
quarter and attach to the sardine 'boat' to resemble a
sail. Attach a small sprig of parsley to each 'sail', to look
like a flag.

PINWHEEL SANDWICHES

These little pinwheels are ideal for younger children as
each is only a mouthful—perfect for a party.

*⅓ cup curd cheese or
   farmer's cheese*
*2 tablespoons snipped
   chives*
*1 tomato, skinned and
   chopped finely*

*4 slices brown bread,
   crusts removed*
1–2 carrots
salt and pepper to taste

Makes about 28
Preparation time:
20 minutes, plus
chilling
Freezing:
Recommended,
without tomato

1. Mix the cheese, chives, tomato, and salt and pepper
together and beat until smooth.
2. Roll the bread lightly with a rolling pin.
3. Cut four 4 × ¼ inch carrot sticks.
4. Spread the bread thickly with the cheese mixture and
place a stick of carrot at one end of each slice. Roll up
firmly like a jelly roll, place in a plastic bag and chill for
1 hour, or until required.
5. Cut each roll into about seven ½ inch slices and
arrange on a plate.

PORCUPINES

Just about anything your children like to eat can be pierced with a cocktail stick and stuck into a grapefruit —try the Roly Polys on page 58: shape the mixture into walnut sized balls, fry in a little oil and serve hot or cold.

1 grapefruit, halved
1 red dessert apple, cored
1 tablespoon lemon juice
2 inch piece cucumber
1/2 cup diced Cheddar
  cheese

1 tomato, cut into wedges
small bunch black grapes
1 large carrot, sliced
  thickly
1 tiny sour gherkin, sliced
TO FINISH:
cocktail sticks

Serves 2
Preparation time:
15 minutes
Freezing:
Not recommended

1. Place each grapefruit half, cut side down, on a plate.
2. Cut the apple into pieces, place in a bowl and sprinkle with the lemon juice. Slice the cucumber thickly and cut each slice into quarters.
3. Thread pieces of apple, cucumber, cheese, tomato, grapes, carrot and gherkin onto cocktail sticks.
4. Press all the filled sticks into the grapefruit to resemble a porcupine.

APPLE COLESLAW

1 red dessert apple, cored
1/3 cup sour cream
1 teaspoon lemon juice
1 cup finely shredded
  white cabbage

1/4 lb black grapes, halved
  and seeded
1 cup alfalfa sprouts or
  1 bunch watercress
salt and pepper to taste

Serves 4
Preparation time:
10 minutes
Freezing:
Not recommended

1. Slice the apple thinly into a bowl, then add the sour cream, lemon juice and salt and pepper. Stir until thoroughly coated to prevent the apple turning brown.
2. Add the cabbage, grapes and cress and toss until the cabbage is well coated. Serve with Shrimp Muffins (page 54) or Roly Polys (page 58).

Note: For older children, you may prefer to add toasted filberts, almonds or sesame seeds.

CARROT SALAD

This is my children's favorite salad—they love it served
with anything.

3 cups finely grated
   carrots
1 tablespoon snipped
   chives
3 tablespoons olive oil

1 tablespoon cider
   vinegar
$1/2$ teaspoon mustard
salt and pepper to taste

1. Place all the ingredients in a bowl and toss thoroughly
until the carrots are well coated. Serve with Scone Pizza
(page 24) or Spicy Sausages (page 26).

Serves 4
Preparation time:
10 minutes
Freezing:
Not recommended

SHRIMP MUFFINS

A special treat for an after-school snack. If you feel that shrimp is too extravagant, or your children don't like it, use ham instead.

½ cup curd cheese or
farmer's cheese
¼ lb medium-size shrimp,
chopped
1 tomato, skinned and
chopped

3 whole wheat or English
muffins, halved and
toasted
½ cup grated Cheddar
cheese
salt and pepper to taste

Serves 3 or 6
Preparation time:
10 minutes
Cooking time:
10 minutes
Freezing:
Not recommended

1. Mix the cheese with the shrimp, tomato, and salt and pepper. Spread over the muffins, then sprinkle with the grated cheese.
2. Place on a baking sheet and bake in a 375°F oven for 10 minutes, until the cheese has melted. Serve immediately, with a salad.

SUNSET EGGS

¾ lb potatoes, peeled
2 tablespoons milk
1 tablespoon snipped
chives
2 teaspoons tomato paste

2 eggs
½ cup grated Cheddar
cheese
salt and pepper to taste

Serves 2
Preparation time:
20 minutes
Cooking time:
20 minutes
Freezing:
Not recommended

1. Boil the potatoes in salted water for about 15 minutes until cooked. Drain thoroughly, mash, then move to one side of the pan and pour in the milk. Heat slightly, then beat thoroughly with a wooden spoon until light and fluffy.
2. Add the chives, tomato paste, and salt and pepper and mix together. Cool slightly, then spoon or pipe into 2 greased individual ovenproof dishes, making a hollow in the center. Break an egg into each hollow and sprinkle with the cheese.
3. Bake in a 400°F oven for 20 minutes, until the egg white is set and the cheese is bubbling. Serve immediately.

BAKED POTATOES

Most children love baked potatoes and the variety of fillings is endless. You can bake the potatoes ahead, then reheat later, or use the microwave oven if you have one.

*2 large potatoes
1 cup grated Cheddar
    cheese
4 scallions, chopped*

*3 tablespoons cream
    cheese beaten with
    3 teaspoons lemon
    juice
salt and pepper to taste*

Serves 4
Preparation time:
10 minutes
Cooking time:
1½ hours
Freezing:
Recommended

1. Make a long slit along one side of each potato and bake in a 400°F oven for 1¼ hours or until cooked.
2. Halve the potatoes lengthways, scoop out the flesh into a bowl and mash with half of the cheese, the scallions, cream cheese mixture, and salt and pepper.
3. Spoon the mixture into the potato shells, sprinkle with the remaining cheese and return to the oven for 15 minutes or until golden. Serve with a salad.

VARIATION
Corn Potatoes. Omit the scallions and mix ⅔ cup cooked whole kernel corn with the potato.

PINTO BAKED BEANS

All children seem to adore baked beans—here's a home-made version without sugar.

*½ lb pinto beans, soaked
    overnight
pinch of salt
1¼ cups tomato sauce
1 teaspoon Dijon
    mustard*

*1 clove garlic, crushed
⅓ cup apple juice
½ teaspoon
    Worcestershire sauce
1 bay leaf*

Serves 4
Preparation time:
5 minutes, plus
soaking time
Cooking time:
50 minutes
Freezing:
Recommended

1. Drain the beans, place in a pan and cover with cold water. Bring to the boil, boil rapidly for 10 minutes, then cover and simmer gently for 25 minutes, adding the salt towards the end of cooking time.
2. Drain and return to the pan with the remaining ingredients. Bring to the boil, cover and simmer gently for 15 minutes. Discard the bay leaf. Serve hot, with whole wheat toast and grated cheese if you wish.

ROLY POLYS

8 oz can red kidney beans, drained	*1 carrot, grated*
2 scallions, chopped	*1 cup whole wheat breadcrumbs*
2 parsley sprigs	*salt and pepper to taste*
1 tablespoon tomato paste	*salad oil for shallow-frying*

Makes about 10
Preparation time:
10 minutes
Cooking time:
3–4 minutes
Freezing:
Recommended

1. Place the beans, scallions, parsley, tomato paste, carrot, half of the breadcrumbs, and salt and pepper in a blender or food processor and work together until smooth.
2. Mold into 'sausages' with dampened hands, then roll in the remaining breadcrumbs to coat.
3. Shallow-fry gently in hot oil for 3–4 minutes, turning once, until golden. Drain on paper towels.
4. Serve hot with pasta shapes tossed in Tomato Sauce (page 37) or Pinto Baked Beans (page 56).

VEGETABLE CRUNCH

⅓ lb cauliflower florets	*¾ cup milk*
1 carrot, sliced thinly	*½ cup grated Cheddar cheese*
½ cup peas	*2 tablespoons whole wheat breadcrumbs*
2 tablespoons margarine	*1 teaspoon sesame seeds*
3 tablespoons whole wheat flour	*salt and pepper to taste*

Serves 2
Preparation time:
10 minutes
Cooking time:
15–20 minutes
Freezing:
Not recommended

1. Cook the cauliflower and carrot in boiling water for 8 minutes, add the peas and cook for 4 minutes. Drain and keep warm.
2. Melt the margarine in a pan, remove from the heat and stir in the flour. Blend in the milk, and salt and pepper, return to the heat and bring to the boil, stirring constantly, until thickened. Cook for 2 minutes, then mix in half of the cheese and the cooked vegetables.
3. Turn into 1 large or 2 individual shallow ovenproof dish(es) and sprinkle with the breadcrumbs, remaining cheese and sesame seeds.
4. Broil for 3–4 minutes, until golden brown and bubbling. Serve immediately.

TOMATO SOUP WITH PIZZA CRACKERS

1 tablespoon salad oil	FOR THE PIZZA
1 onion, chopped	CRACKERS:
1 carrot, chopped	2 tablespoons tomato
2 celery sticks, chopped	paste
14 oz can tomatoes,	1/2–1 teaspoon
chopped	Worcestershire
1/4 lb potato, chopped	sauce
1 clove garlic, chopped	1/2 teaspoon dried
1 bay leaf	oregano
2 tablespoons tomato	1 clove garlic, crushed
paste	2–3 English muffins,
1 teaspoon honey	halved
3 cups vegetable stock or	1/2 cup grated cheese
water	TO SERVE (optional):
salt and pepper	little yogurt or whipping
	cream

Serves 4–6
Preparation time:
20 minutes
Cooking time:
35 minutes
Freezing:
Recommended,
for the soup only

1. Heat the oil in a large pan, add the onion and cook until softened. Add the remaining ingredients, cover and simmer gently for 35 minutes.
2. Cool slightly, discard the bay leaf, then puree in a food processor or blender. Return to the pan and keep warm while making the pizza crackers.
3. Blend the tomato paste with the Worcestershire sauce, oregano and garlic and spread thinly over each muffin half. Sprinkle with the grated cheese and broil for 1–2 minutes. Cool slightly.
4. Drizzle a little yogurt or cream on top of the soup, if you wish. Serve with the pizza crackers.

CORN SOUP WITH CHEESE ROLLS

2 tablespoons salad oil	2 strips bacon
1 onion, chopped	salt and pepper to taste
2 tablespoons whole	FOR THE CHEESE ROLLS:
wheat flour	2 small whole wheat soft
3 3/4 cups milk	rolls, halved
1/2 lb potato, diced	2 teaspoons mustard
1 bay leaf	1/2 cup grated Cheddar
1 celery stick, chopped	cheese
2 cups frozen whole	
kernel corn	
2 tablespoons chopped	
parsley	

1. Heat in the oil in a pan, add the onion and fry until softened. Remove from the heat, mix in the flour, then gradually stir in the milk.
2. Bring to the boil, stirring constantly, then add the remaining ingredients, except the bacon. Simmer gently for 20–25 minutes, until the potatoes are cooked. Discard the bay leaf.
3. Meanwhile, broil the bacon until crisp and make the cheese rolls: spread the rolls with mustard, sprinkle with the cheese and broil until brown and bubbling.
4. Sprinkle the bacon over the soup and serve with the cheese rolls.

Serves 4
Preparation time: 15 minutes
Cooking time: 20–25 minutes
Freezing: Recommended at end of stage 2

WHOLE WHEAT BISCUIT SHAPES

Most children won't be able to resist these novelty-shaped biscuits. They are so quick to make you could serve them fresh from the oven when they come home from school. Delicious with a sweet or savory spread (see below and opposite).

*2 cups whole wheat flour
   sifted with 3 teaspoons
   baking powder
1/4 cup margarine*

*1/2 cup milk
   (approximately)
1/4 teaspoon sesame
   seeds
milk to glaze*

Makes about 15
Preparation time:
15 minutes
Cooking time:
12–15 minutes
Freezing:
Recommended

1. Place the flour, margarine and milk in a mixing bowl and mix with a fork to form a soft dough; add a little more milk if necessary.
2. Turn onto a lightly floured surface, knead lightly and roll out to a 3/4 inch thickness. Using a 2 inch shaped cutter (e.g. star, animal) cut out about 15 biscuits.
3. Place on a floured baking sheet, brush with milk and sprinkle with the sesame seeds.
4. Bake in a 425°F oven for 12–15 minutes. Cool on a rack. Serve warm or cold.

APRICOT SPREAD

Use this spread in place of jam on bread, biscuits, as a filling for layer cakes, etc. For a change add 1/4 cup toasted chopped almonds.

*1/2 cup chopped dried
   apricots*

3/4 cup orange juice

Makes about
1 cup
Preparation time:
10 minutes
Cooking time:
20 minutes
Freezing:
Recommended

1. Place the apricots and orange juice in a small pan, cover and simmer gently for 20 minutes, until tender.
2. Puree in a food processor or blender, turn into a clean jar, seal and store in the refrigerator for up to 2 weeks.

VARIATION
Prune Spread. Follow the instructions above, using pitted prunes instead of apricots and water instead of orange juice.

PEANUT AND CELERY SPREAD

An interesting spread to serve when the kids want something different. If your children like spicy flavors, add a little ground red pepper and coriander after softening the onion and celery and fry for 1 minute.

1 tablespoon salad oil
1 onion, chopped finely
2 celery sticks, chopped
¼ cup crunchy peanut
  butter

⅓ cup water
2 teaspoons soy sauce
  (preferably Japanese)
1 teaspoon lemon juice

1. Heat the oil in a pan, add the onion and celery and fry until softened. Mix in the peanut butter, then gradually blend in the water, stirring until thickened. Add the soy sauce and lemon juice and leave to cool.
2. Turn into a clean jar, seal and store in the refrigerator for up to 5 days.

Makes about 1 lb
Preparation time:
10 minutes
Cooking time:
5 minutes
Freezing:
Recommended

VARIATION
Peanut and Celery Dip.   Add a little tomato juice to thin the mixture slightly and serve with vegetable sticks.

POPCORN

The kids love to help you with this. Don't lift the lid of the pan until most of the popping has stopped, or the popcorn will go everywhere. For a savory version, omit the honey and sprinkle with a little salt.

1 tablespoon corn oil   *1 tablespoon honey*
1 oz popping corn

Serves 4
Preparation time:
5 minutes
Cooking time:
2 minutes
Freezing:
Not recommended

1. Heat the oil in a large, heavy-based pan with a lid. Add the popping corn, cover and cook, shaking the pan constantly, until the kernels have popped.
2. Transfer to a bowl and pour over the honey. Mix thoroughly until coated. Serve cold.

VARIATION
Honey Clusters. After popping the corn, remove from the pan and set aside. Add 2 tablespoons honey to the pan and boil for 30 seconds. Quickly stir in the popcorn until evenly coated. Cool slightly, then form the mixture into 16 small balls and leave to set.

CHEESE AND TOMATO STRAWS

The same dough can also be used to make savory crackers, using animal or other cutters.

1 cup whole wheat   *1 egg yolk*
*   flour*   *2–3 teaspoons cold*
¼ cup margarine   *   water*
¾ cup coarsely grated   *2 tablespoons tomato*
*   Cheddar cheese*   *   paste*

Makes about 80
Preparation time:
30 minutes
Cooking time:
8–10 minutes
Freezing:
Recommended

1. Place the flour in a bowl and rub in the margarine until the mixture resembles breadcrumbs. Stir in the cheese.
2. Mix the egg yolk, water and tomato paste together, add to the flour mixture and mix to a firm dough.
3. Turn onto a lightly floured surface and knead lightly until smooth. Roll out thinly into a 9 inch square, then cut into 3 × ¼ inch strips.
4. Place on a baking sheet and bake in a 400°F oven for 8–10 minutes, until golden. Cool on a rack.

PINWHEELS

Popular little savory snacks to serve after school, in lunch boxes or just as a nibble to replace candy.

*½ lb frozen whole wheat
    puff pastry, thawed*
*1 tablespoon yeast
    extract*

½ teaspoon water
*1 cup grated Cheddar
    cheese*

1. Roll out the pastry thinly on a lightly floured surface to a rectangle measuring 10 × 12 inches.
2. Mix the yeast extract and water together until blended, spread over the pastry to cover completely, then sprinkle with the cheese.
3. Roll up loosely from one short side like a jelly roll. Chill for 20 minutes.
4. Cut into ¼ inch slices and place on a baking sheet. Bake in a 400°F oven for 10–12 minutes until golden. Cool on a rack.

Makes about 35
Preparation time:
15 minutes
Cooking time:
10–12 minutes
Freezing:
Not recommended

BANANA CAKE

½ cup spreadable
  margarine
¼ cup honey
2 ripe bananas, mashed
2 eggs
1 cup whole wheat flour
  sifted with 2 teaspoons
  baking powder

FOR THE FILLING:
1 small banana, mashed
  with 1 teaspoon lemon
  juice
¼ cup curd cheese or
  farmer's cheese
2 tablespoons ground
  almonds
1 teaspoon honey

Makes one cake
Preparation time:
15 minutes
Cooking time:
20–25 minutes
Freezing:
Recommended,
without the filling

1. Grease and line two 7 inch round cake pans.
2. Place the margarine, honey and bananas in a bowl and blend with a fork. Add the eggs and flour, and beat together thoroughly until smooth.
3. Turn into the prepared pans and bake in a 350°F oven for 20–25 minutes, until the cakes are springy to the touch. Cool on a rack.
4. To make the filling, mix all the ingredients together until smooth. Use to sandwich the cakes together. This cake is best eaten within 48 hours.

BANANA BROWNIES

3 oz unsweetened carob
  or baker's semi-sweet
  chocolate, in pieces
¼ cup corn oil
¼ cup honey

1 cup whole wheat flour
  sifted with 1½ tea-
  spoons baking powder
2 tablespoons cold water
1 banana, mashed
2 eggs

Makes about 16
Preparation time:
15 minutes
Cooking time:
25–30 minutes
Freezing:
Recommended

1. Grease and line a 7 inch square shallow cake pan.
2. Place the carob or chocolate pieces, oil and honey in a small pan and heat gently until melted.
3. Place the flour in a mixing bowl and make a well in the center. Beat in the carob or chocolate mixture with the water, banana and eggs until smooth.
4. Pour into the prepared pan and bake in a 350°F oven for 25–30 minutes, until just beginning to shrink from the sides of the pan.
5. Cool on a rack. Cut into small pieces to serve.

CAROB CUP CAKES

These look just like little chocolate cakes, but as carob is naturally sweet, they contain far less sugar. The flavor is slightly different from chocolate, but still delicious. If you prefer, cocoa and chocolate can be substituted for the carob powder and bar. It is a quick and easy recipe that older children will enjoy making themselves.

1/4 cup dark brown sugar, packed
2 eggs
1/2 cup sunflower oil
1/2 cup water
1 rounded tablespoon malt extract
1 1/2 cups whole wheat flour sifted with 2 teaspoons baking powder

1/4 cup carob powder
FOR THE TOPPING:
1/4 cup curd cheese or farmer's cheese
1 oz unsweetened carob bar, melted
grated rind of 1 orange

Makes about 15
Preparation time:
25 minutes
Cooking time:
15 minutes
Freezing:
Recommended

1. Place the sugar, eggs, oil, water and malt extract in a bowl and mix together thoroughly.
2. Sift in the flour and carob powder and beat until smooth.
3. Arrange 12 paper cupcake cases on a baking sheet and fill each one three-quarters full. Bake in a 350°F oven for 15 minutes. Cool on a rack.
4. To make the topping, beat the cheese in a bowl until smooth. Add the melted carob and orange rind and beat thoroughly. Place in a piping bag fitted with a large fluted tip and pipe a rosette onto each cake, or spread using a knife.

GINGERBREAD

Store this cake in an airtight container for several days before eating to let the flavor mellow and the cake become moister.

2 cups whole wheat flour
4 teaspoons ground ginger
1 teaspoon each ground mixed spice and baking soda
1/2 cup sunflower oil

1/4 cup molasses
1/3 cup honey
2/3 cup apple juice
2 eggs, beaten
2 tablespoons slivered almonds (optional)

1. Grease and line a 7 inch square cake pan.
2. Place the flour in a mixing bowl, then sift in the spices and baking soda.
3. Make a well in the center and add the oil, molasses, honey, apple juice and eggs. Beat thoroughly, gradually incorporating the flour until smooth.
4. Turn into the prepared pan and sprinkle with the almonds if using.
5. Bake in a 325°F oven for 1–1¼ hours, until a skewer pierced through the center of the cake comes out clean.
6. Leave in the pan for 5 minutes, then turn onto a rack to cool. Cut into slices to serve.

Makes one cake
Preparation time:
20 minutes
Cooking time:
1–1¼ hours
Freezing:
Recommended

SHORTBREAD FACES

2 tablespoons dark brown
    sugar, packed
1/4 cup margarine
3/4 cup whole wheat flour

few currants
2 glacé cherries
little angelica

Makes about 10
Preparation time:
15 minutes
Cooking time:
15 minutes
Freezing:
Recommended

1. Beat the sugar and margarine until light and fluffy. Add the flour and mix until the mixture binds together.
2. Turn onto a floured surface and knead until smooth. Roll out thinly, then cut into circles using a 3 inch round cutter. Shape and press in currants, cherries and angelica for eyes, nose and mouth.
3. Bake in a 325°F oven for 15 minutes. Leave to cool on the baking sheet.

GINGERBREAD MEN

Glacé icing is usually used to decorate these cookies, but curd cheese or farmer's cheese gives just as good a result. Don't pipe them too far in advance or the cheese will discolor.

1 cup whole wheat flour
1/2 teaspoon each baking
    soda and ground
    cinnamon
1 teaspoon ground
    ginger
2 tablespoons margarine

1/4 cup dark brown sugar,
    packed
1 tablespoon honey
1 teaspoon orange juice
TO DECORATE:
1/4 cup curd cheese or
    farmer's cheese
little milk to mix

Makes 12–14
Preparation time:
20 minutes
Cooking time:
10–15 minutes
Freezing:
Recommended,
without
decoration

1. Place the flour in a mixing bowl and sift in the baking soda and spices.
2. Place the margarine, sugar and honey in a pan and heat gently, stirring, until melted. Cool, then pour onto the flour with the orange juice and mix to a firm dough.
3. Turn onto a floured surface and roll out to about 1/4 inch thick. Using a gingerbread man cutter, cut out 12–14 men and place on greased baking sheets.
4. Bake in a 325°F oven for 10–15 minutes, until firm. Cool on a rack.
5. Mix the cheese with a little milk to give a smooth consistency. Spoon into a waxed paper piping bag fitted with a writing tip and pipe eyes, nose, mouth and buttons on each man.

CAROB CRACKLES

Any finely chopped nuts can be used instead of sesame
seeds, if you prefer. I suggest that you brown them
first—it really does improve the 'nutty' flavor.

2 tablespoons honey
2 tablespoons margarine
4 oz unsweetened carob
 bar or baker's semi-
 sweet chocolate, chopped

6 cups bran flakes
2 tablespoons sesame seeds,
 toasted

1. Place the honey, margarine and carob or chocolate in
a pan and heat gently, stirring, until melted.
2. Add the bran flakes and sesame seeds and mix
thoroughly until well coated. Spoon into paper cake
cases and leave to set.

Makes 10–12
Preparation time:
10 minutes
Freezing:
Not recommended

PEANUT COOKIES

These crisp little cookies are very high in fiber. They can be served without the melted chocolate, if you prefer.

1/4 cup salad oil
1/4 cup peanut butter
1/4 cup dark brown sugar, packed
1 egg
1/4 cup rolled oats
3/4 cup whole wheat flour

1 teaspoon baking powder
1/2 cup chopped peanuts, browned
4 oz baker's semi-sweet chocolate, melted, to decorate (optional)

Makes 16
Preparation time: 30 minutes
Cooking time: 12–15 minutes
Freezing: Recommended

1. Place the oil, peanut butter and sugar in a pan and heat gently, stirring, until blended. Add the remaining ingredients and mix together thoroughly.
2. Place teaspoonfuls of the mixture a little apart on a greased baking sheet and flatten with a dampened fork. Bake in a 350°F oven for 12–15 minutes, until firm. Transfer to a rack.
3. Spoon the melted chocolate on top of the biscuits and mark into wavy lines with a fork to decorate, if you wish. Leave to set.

CAROB CHIP COOKIES

Use other nuts, if you prefer, and you can use chocolate chips instead of the carob.

1/3 cup margarine
1/4 cup dark brown sugar, packed
1 egg
1 cup whole wheat flour

1 teaspoon baking powder, sifted
3 oz unsweetened carob bar, chopped
1/2 cup chopped filberts, browned

Makes about 20
Preparation time: 15 minutes
Cooking time: 15–20 minutes
Freezing: Recommended

1. Cream the margarine and sugar together until light and fluffy, then add the egg and beat thoroughly. Add the remaining ingredients and blend together.
2. Place teaspoonfuls of the mixture a little apart on a greased baking sheet and flatten with a dampened fork. Bake in a 350°F oven for 15–20 minutes, until golden. Cool on a rack.

ALMOND CANDY

Any dried fruits can be used for this delicious candy. The coating can also be varied—try toasted sesame seeds, coconut or grated carob.

²/₃ cup pitted dates
¹/₃ cup dried apricots
¹/₃ cup raisins

2 tablespoons apple juice
¹/₃ cup chopped almonds, browned

1. Place the dates, apricots, raisins and apple juice in a food processor or blender and work together until smooth, scraping down the sides as necessary.
2. Form the mixture into balls the size of a cherry, then roll them in the almonds until completely coated.

Makes 30
Preparation time: 15 minutes
Freezing: Recommended

DRINKS

WATERMELON CRUSH

½ lb slice watermelon
3 tablespoons grape
  juice

1 egg white
1¼ cups water
2 ice cubes

Makes about
2 cups
Preparation time:
5 minutes
Freezing:
Not recommended

1. Remove the skin from the watermelon, scoop out the seeds and chop the flesh.
2. Place in a food processor or blender with the remaining ingredients and work together for 20 seconds until smooth.
3. Pour into glasses and serve immediately.

LEMON BARLEY WATER

An extremely refreshing and thirst-quenching drink.

2 oz pearl barley
2½ cups water
pared rind and juice of
  1 lemon

1½ tablespoons honey
lemon slices to serve

Makes about
2 cups
Preparation time:
5 minutes, plus
chilling
Cooking time:
25 minutes
Freezing:
Recommended

1. Place the pearl barley in a sieve, then pour over boiling water to clean it; this ensures the finished drink will be clear.
2. Place the barley, cold water and lemon rind in a pan, cover and simmer for 25 minutes.
3. Strain into a pitcher, then add the lemon juice and honey. Float lemon slices on top and serve chilled, within 24 hours.

ORANGE FLOAT

1¼ cups orange juice
1¼ cups carbonated
  mineral water

4 scoops Orange and
  Honey Ice Cream
  (page 44)

Serves 4
Preparation time:
5 minutes
Freezing:
Not recommended

1. Mix the orange juice and mineral water together and pour into 4 tall glasses.
2. Place a scoop of ice cream in each glass to serve.

STRAWBERRY YOGURT SHAKE

A quick and healthy summer drink. Any soft fruits can be substituted for the strawberries.

¼ cup orange juice, chilled
⅔ cup plain yogurt, chilled

½ cup strawberries
1 tablespoon honey

Serves 2–3
Preparation time:
2 minutes
Freezing:
Not recommended

1. Place the orange juice and yogurt in a food processor or blender. Add the strawberries and honey and work together for 20 seconds until smooth.
2. Pour into glasses and serve with straws.

BANANA MILK SHAKE

Milk shakes can be made in many different flavors —simply replace the banana with soft fruits of your choice. If you use a very ripe banana, omit the honey.

1¼ cups milk
1 ripe banana, chopped

1 teaspoon honey

Serves 2
Preparation time:
2 minutes
Freezing:
Not recommended

1. Place all the ingredients in a food processor or blender and work for 15 seconds, until smooth.
2. Pour into tall glasses; serve immediately, with straws.

HOT CAROB FOAM

Serve immediately, or the foam will disappear!

1¼ cups hot milk
1 oz unsweetened carob bar or baker's semi-sweet chocolate, grated

1 teaspoon honey
¼ teaspoon ground cinnamon

Serves 2
Preparation time:
2 minutes
Freezing:
Not recommended

1. Place all the ingredients in a food processor or blender and work together until smooth.
2. Pour into mugs and sprinkle with a little more cinnamon. Serve immediately.

VARIATION
Iced Minty Milk. Replace cinnamon with a few drops peppermint extract. Serve cold with ice cubes.

BUNNY CUP

An excellent and delicious way to introduce vegetables
to a child who won't eat them in their usual guise.

2 carrots, chopped
1 celery stick, chopped
²/₃ cup water
²/₃ cup tomato juice

¹/₂–1 teaspoon
  Worcestershire sauce
1 teaspoon lemon
  juice
salt and pepper to taste

1. Place the carrots, celery and water in a food processor or blender and work together for 30 seconds
until smooth.
2. Strain, pressing through as much juice as possible,
then stir in the remaining ingredients.
3. Pour into 2 glasses to serve.

Serves 2
Preparation time:
5 minutes
Freezing:
Recommended

COCONUT SLUSH

If you prefer the drink to be thinner, leave at room temperature for 5–10 minutes before blending.

⅓ cup unsweetened
*   flaked coconut*
¼ cup boiling water

1¼ cups milk
2 teaspoons honey

Serves 2
Preparation time:
10 minutes
Freezing time:
About 2 hours

1. Blend the coconut with the boiling water, strain after 10 minutes. Mix in the milk and honey.
2. Turn into a rigid freezerproof container, cover and freeze for about 2 hours, until half frozen.
3. Turn into a food processor or blender and work for 5–10 seconds until smooth. Pour into glasses.

APPLE FIZZ

2½ cups apple juice
1½ cups carbonated
*   mineral water*

1 red dessert apple, cored
*   and sliced*
mint sprigs to decorate

Serves 6
Preparation time:
5 minutes
Freezing:
Not recommended

1. Place the apple juice in a pitcher and add the mineral water.
2. Divide the apple slices between 6 glasses, pour in the apple fizz and decorate with mint sprigs.

FROZEN FRUIT POPS

You can make these out of any soft fruits in season, or simply use fresh fruit juice.

½ cup raspberries
⅔ cup water
1 tablespoon honey

2 tablespoons grape
*   juice*

Makes about 8
Preparation time:
10 minutes
Freezing time:
3 hours

1. Place the raspberries and water in a food processor or blender and work for 20 seconds until smooth.
2. Strain into a pitcher, then stir in the honey and grape juice.
3. Pour into about 8 ice-pop molds, depending on size, and freeze for 3 hours, until solid.

CREAMY POPS

My children particularly like banana pops, but you could substitute strawberries or any other soft fruits in season, adjusting the amount of honey to taste.

²/₃ cup milk　　　　　*1 ripe banana*
²/₃ cup plain yogurt　　*2 teaspoons honey*

1. Place all the ingredients in a food processor or blender and work together for 20 seconds until smooth.
2. Pour into about 12 ice-pop molds, depending on size, and freeze for 3 hours, until solid.

Makes about 12
Preparation time:
10 minutes
Freezing time:
3 hours

INDEX

Photography by: Clive Streeter
Designed by: Sue Storey
Home economist: Carole Handslip
Stylist: Sue Russell
Illustration by: Linda Smith
U.S. Consultant Editor: Carla Capalbo